THE ASHMOLEAN MUSEUM
OXFORD

D0300788

Prestel

Munich · London · New York

PRÆMIA
HONORARIA.

Contents

opposite: John Riley (1646–91), *Elias Ashmole, c.* 1681, founder of the Ashmolean Museum.

The Ashmolean, founded in 1683, is the oldest museum in Great Britain and one of the oldest in the world. Its long and distinguished history is expertly outlined in this guidebook by Arthur MacGregor. It has immensely rich and very diverse collections – Egyptian Predynastic maceheads, Cycladic figurines, Greek vases, English medieval pottery, drawings by Raphael, Chinese ceramics, Pre-Raphaelite paintings, to name only a few – and can justifiably claim to be the most important museum in this country outside London. In this book we have identified some of the highlights of the collections, but only a visit will enable you to do justice to the Ashmolean. These treasures belong to the University of Oxford and the Museum is a major resource for teaching and research in the University. The Ashmolean is also a great public museum, open six days a week with free admission, serving a large local, national and international audience. Currently the Museum attracts 250,000 visitors a year, but we hope that an imaginative programme of temporary exhibitions and educational activities, as well as increased access to the remarkable riches of the permanent collections via an expanded range of publications and the Museum's website, will raise this figure.

A museum which no longer acquires works of art is a dead museum. The Ashmolean is constantly adding to its collections, and a number of important recent acquisitions, including a major portrait by Titian, a terracotta bust by Rysbrack, a twelfth-century Chinese bodhisattva, an Anglo-Saxon cross and a Khmer sculpture, are included here. We are especially grateful for help given by the Heritage Lottery Fund and the National Art Collections Fund as well as by our active and generous Friends.

October 2000 sees the opening of the Khoan and Michael Sullivan Gallery of Chinese Painting. In this fine new space, by the architects Van Heyningen and Haward, we will at last be able to do justice to the Museum's great holdings of Chinese paintings, largely acquired through the generosity of the Reyes family in 1995. Early in 2001 the new gallery of twentieth-century art opens and our early twentieth-century British paintings – notably by Sickert, Nash and Spencer – will be placed, with the sculpture collections, along-side Picasso, Matisse and Braque. This is an exciting period in the Ashmolean's development and I hope you find your visit stimulating and enjoyable.

Dr Christopher Brown
Director   September 2000

Titian (c. 1487–1576), *Portrait of Giacomo Doria.* This portrait, purchased in July 2000, shows Giacomo di Agostino Doria, a Genoese merchant living in Venice during the 1530s. Titian, who dominated Venetian art during its greatest period, was previously represented in the Museum's collection by a single chalk drawing. The acquisition of the painting was made possible through the generosity of the Heritage Lottery Fund, the National Art Collections Fund and the Friends of the Ashmolean.

By the time the Duke of York presided over the official opening of the Ashmolean Museum, on 21 May 1683, a large part of the collection housed in this novel institution – 'the first public museum in England' – already had a history stretching back over half a century. The Duke, who succeeded to the throne within two years as James II, might have spared a thought for the founder of the collection, the lively, personable and adventurous John Tradescant (d. 1638, Fig. 1), appointed to the royal household under Charles I and already the familiar of some of the most influential of James I's courtiers in the earliest decades of the seventeenth century.

Fig. 1. Attributed to Emanuel de Critz (1608–65), *Posthumous portrait of John Tradescant the Elder*, possibly 1650s.

Tradescant's career had developed from obscure beginnings through a series of appointments as gardener to the 1st Earl of Salisbury at Hatfield House, to the scholar and diplomat Lord (Edward) Wotton at St Augustine's Palace, Canterbury, and then to the all-powerful George Villiers, 1st Duke of Buckingham. These successive posts had provided Tradescant with valuable opportunities for travel, notably to the Netherlands and France in 1611, to Archangel in 1618 and to the western Mediterranean in 1620-21; his last known overseas adventure was in the company of the Duke of Buckingham in 1627, on the latter's disastrous expedition to the Île de Ré, off La Rochelle.

On each of these occasions Tradescant took care to acquire not only such exotic plants as he could lay hands on, which he nurtured in his garden and distributed to like-minded botanists and gardeners, but also man-made and natural rarities of every kind, destined for his cabinet of curiosities. More such material reached him through overseas merchants, adventurers and diplomats, especially those within the circle of the Duke of Buckingham, who appears to have been notably indulgent towards his gardener. When his master was assassinated in 1628, Tradescant bought himself a roomy house at Lambeth where he installed his family, established a garden of exotic plants (many of them introduced for the first time to England) and founded the museum whose encyclopaedic character earned it the epithet by which it is known to posterity – 'The Ark'.

Although later appointed Keeper of His Majesty's Gardens, Vines and Silkworms at Oatlands Palace in Surrey (and ultimately, in 1637, first curator of the newly established Botanic Garden at Oxford – a post which he did not live to take up), Tradescant was to maintain The Ark, assisted by his son John (1608–62, Fig. 2), also a gardener by profession who reached his thirtieth birthday in the year of his father's death in 1638. The younger Tradescant proceeded, in his own words, 'with continued diligence' to augment and preserve 'those Rarities and Curiosities which my Father had scedulously collected'. Perhaps his most important contributions would have arrived as a result of three visits he made to Virginia

Fig. 2. Attributed to Thomas de Critz (1607–53), *John Tradescant the Younger* (on left) *with Roger Friend*, 1645, with exotic sea-shells from the Tradescant museum.

between 1637 and 1654. These new trophies were quickly made accessible (for a fee) to the public that flocked to see The Ark. This was itself a significant step in the history of collections, for up to that point the formation of privately owned cabinets of curiosities had been an activity limited to the higher echelons of society, placing them within the exclusive reach of those with an appropriate social standing: the Tradescant museum broke this mould and opened the era of public museum-going in England. Already in 1634 a well-travelled visitor, on home leave from the East India Company, could write of a visit to Tradescant's museum that he had 'spent that whole day in peruseinge, and that superficially, such as he had gathered together ... soe that I am almost perswaded a Man might in one daye behold and collect into one place more Curiosities than he s[h]ould see if hee spent all his life in Travell'. Four years later, a more detailed account of the collection by a visiting German makes the earliest mention of what remains the jewel of the collection, *Powhatan's Mantle* (Fig. 3).

In 1650 Tradescant received the first of several visits from Elias Ashmole (1617–92, see frontispiece), a lawyer by profession and an antiquary and genealogist by inclination, who would later rise to become Comptroller of the Excise and Windsor Herald. With Ashmole's encouragement, assistance and financial backing, a

Fig. 3. *Powhatan's Mantle*, 235 x 160 cm. The centre-piece of the surviving Tradescant collection, first mentioned in 1638 as 'the robe of the King of Virginia'. Made of four deerskins and decorated with shells, it was most probably a hanging rather than a garment. Its association in the early 17th century with Powhatan (the father of Pocahontas) remains perfectly likely.

Fig. 4. Michael Burghers, *The Ashmolean Museum*, *c.* 1685. The view shows the east front of the 'Old Ashmolean', built by a local mason, Thomas Wood.

catalogue of the collection was published in 1656, with the title *Musæum Tradescantianum*; it was to prove so popular that a second edition was produced in 1660. In gratitude Tradescant drew up a deed of gift by which the entire collection was made over to Ashmole, the deed to be enacted after the death of Tradescant himself and that of his wife, Hester. In the event, Ashmole had to resort to the courts in order to secure his inheritance from Hester, but it was this collection, augmented by elements of Ashmole's own coin cabinet and his library of books and manuscripts, which he was to offer to the University of Oxford. An express condition of Ashmole's gift was that the University for its part should build an appropriate 'repository' in which to house it (Fig. 4), and it was here, adjacent to the Sheldonian Theatre in Broad Street, that the Ashmolean Museum received its formal inauguration in 1683.

The previous fifty years had seen a considerable expansion of Tradescant's miscellaneous cabinet of curiosities as well as a trans-formation in perceptions of its significance. While it was still at Lambeth it had already become the resort of naturalists such as John Ray and Thomas Johnson, eager to examine the zoological and botanical rarities that could scarcely be found elsewhere in England, and it was the scientific utility of the collection that Ashmole stressed in the statutes he drew up for the governance of his new foundation:

> Because the knowledge of Nature is very necessarie to
> humaine life, health, & the conveniences thereof, & because
> that knowledge cannot be soe well & usefully attain'd, except
> the history of Nature be knowne & considered ... I have
> amass'd together great variety of naturall Concretes & Bodies,
> & bestowed them on the University of Oxford...

The newly founded Ashmolean was presided over by Dr Robert
Plot (keeper 1683–90), a natural scientist and the University's first
professor of chemistry. Having supervised the transfer of Ashmole's
benefaction to Oxford in March 1683 (when the arrival of twelve
cart-loads of material was recorded), Plot set about installing it.
The collection itself was confined to the uppermost of the building's three floors, the basement level being fitted out as a chemical
laboratory (the first such facility within the University) and the
ground floor being taken up by offices and the 'School of Natural
History'; all three elements were conceived as forming a single,
unified institution, integrated under Plot's control. As such it
formed the first successful expression of an academic ideal whose
origins can be traced back to the works of Francis Bacon and
which coloured the activities of the recently founded Royal
Society, of which Plot was an influential Fellow: in keeping with
its founder's vision, it was the Museum's role as the centre of scientific life in the University that was considered paramount during
this period.

There is evidence for much industry in the Ashmolean during
its early years, with Plot and his assistant, Edward Lhwyd, cata-
loguing the complete collection and seeing to its administration
according to the rigorous series of statutes drawn up by Ashmole.
By the time Lhwyd succeeded to the keepership on Plot's retire-
ment, he too had built up a considerable scientific reputation, particularly in the nascent field of palaeontology; during his regime
the reputation of the institution remained high, although Lhwyd's
prolonged absences in the field placed its smooth administration
under considerable strain. His successor, David Parry (keeper
1709–14) did little to improve matters: although a good scholar, it
seems he was generally to be found 'lounging about in the inns, so
that one scarcely ever meets him in the Museum'. The mathemati-
cian John Whiteside (keeper 1714–29) did much to repair the inte-
grity of the three-part Ashmolean, but under those who followed

him the links between its constituent elements were progressively dissolved, much to the detriment of the exhibition galleries, which found themselves increasingly isolated and struggling to maintain their relevance.

A vivid cameo of the Museum and its visiting public survives from the period of Parry's keepership, recorded in the diary of a youthful German traveller, Zacharias Conrad von Uffenbach. When he called at the Ashmolean in 1710, the earnest Grand Tourist was frankly appalled: 'The specimens in the museum might ... be much better arranged and preserved', he complained, although '... it is surprising that things are preserved even as well as they are, since the people impetuously handle every thing in the usual English fashion and ... even the women are allowed up here for sixpence; they run here and there, grabbing at everything and taking no rebuff from the *sub-custos*'. Such a chaotic situation indicates that Ashmole's statutes, in which it had been decreed 'That the Rarities shall be shewed but to one Company at a tyme, & that upon their being entred into the Musaeum, the dore shall be shut', were being widely ignored. Records from the period confirm that, in addition to its scholarly and genteel visitors, the Museum proved popular with a wide section of ordinary people including servants, country folk and bargees passing along the Thames – exactly the kind of society that so scandalised von Uffenbach, who clearly felt they had no place in a learned milieu.

By mid-century the keepership of the Ashmolean had degenerated into little more than a sinecure, then held by Dr George Huddesford, president of Trinity College. The effects of such an arrangement were rendered all too obvious in the Museum, where the collections '... lay in the utmost confusion. Lhwyd's fossils were tumbled out of their papers, and nobody regarded or understood them'. Several potential benefactors turned away from the Museum at this time, deeply unwilling to entrust their own cherished collections to the tender mercies of such a blatantly cynical regime. When Huddesford's twenty-three-year-old son William inherited the post in 1755, the entire future of the institution must have seemed to hang in the balance. In the event, the younger Huddesford wrought a transformation on the museum element that was little short of miraculous, redisplaying, recataloguing and generally revitalising the exhibits. By the end of William's first year in office he received a letter from a prominent London antiquary which captures the new spirit of optimism generated by his appointment: 'I cannot help expressing the Pleasure I have in hearing that you earnestly apply yourself to Digesting into some order the confus'd heap of natural Bodies which are under your Care at the Musaeum ... Tis the only means by which it can increase and become an honour to the University, instead of being the contempt of Strangers.' Benefactions began to flow again and the contemporary catalogues bear witness to the many gifts attracted by the direct example of the dedicated and industrious keeper.

One result of Huddesford's comprehensive review of the collections was the highlighting of the inexorable decay that had taken its toll – particularly on the natural history collections – since the Museum's foundation. Many specimens were by now too far gone to be saved and were formally removed from the collections. The most spectacular casualty of this process was Tradescant's stuffed dodo, which evidently had reached such an advanced state of decomposition that it had to be removed from display in 1755; today only its comparatively indestructible head and one of its feet survive. While rot (due to the very imperfect methods of taxidermy available at the time) and infestations of pests took their toll on the zoological exhibits, even the mineral specimens were not immune to decay, promoted by the sulphurous atmosphere generated by the Museum's open coal fires.

Following the positive interlude of William Huddesford's keepership which ended in 1772, the Ashmolean relapsed into another half-century of comparative stagnation, during which time the most noteworthy event was the arrival in 1776 of an important consignment of ethnographic material collected in the South Seas on Captain Cook's second voyage of discovery and presented to the Museum by Johann Reinhold Forster and his son George. The Forsters had accompanied the *Resolution* in the capacity of naturalists and had expected to be fully involved in publishing the results of the expedition; in 1776, however, Reinhold fell out with the Admiralty, which may help to explain his benefaction to Oxford, where he already had many friends and had received the honorary degree of DCL (Doctor of Civil Law). With regard to the Museum, it seems symptomatic of the torpor into which its curators had fallen that the gift made no recorded impact whatever in the registers: it was never catalogued at Oxford, although the Forsters' hand-list, compiled to accompany the benefaction, still survives (along with the objects themselves) in the Pitt Rivers Museum, making it the best-documented collection of 'second voyage' material known to present-day ethnographers. If the objects were displayed at all (and they may, in fact, have spent much time in storage), it seems likely that they were exhibited in premises apart from the Ashmolean itself.

New and fundamental reforms were imposed on the somnambulant institution under the brothers John and Philip Duncan, who held the keepership successively from 1823 to 1854. Both were adherents of the tenets of Natural Theology, dedicated to the revelation of 'evidences' of the divine nature of all creation through the study of natural history. The movement already had several influential supporters in the academic community, including William Buckland, Professor of Mineralogy, and John Kidd, Regius Professor of Medicine, both of whom gave lecture courses in the Museum basement during the earlier part of the Duncans' regime. In a systematic manner, the Duncans replanned the entire display as an exposition of this philosophy: the texts of several of their labels are preserved, liberally interspersed with lengthy, verbatim

Fig. 5. The newly displayed ground-floor gallery of the 'Old Ashmolean', engraving from the Museum's printed catalogue of 1836.

W.A.Delamotte. del

O.JEWITT. sc

THE LOWER ROOM OF THE MUSEUM.

passages quoted directly from the works of one of the movement's most influential thinkers, William Paley. At this period the displays expanded into the ground-floor level of the Museum building: the frontispiece from the descriptive catalogue which the Duncans published in 1836 provides our earliest visual record of the interior, as redisplayed at this time (Fig. 5). Those elements of the collection which failed to find a place in the Duncans' didactic programme – that is to say, almost all the works of man as opposed to God – were consigned at this time to a small ancillary room, to the walls of the staircase, or to storage, so as not to interrupt the thrust of the primary message.

Under the Duncans' galvanising influence, the Ashmolean attracted a flood of new benefactions, particularly in their favoured field of zoology. On taking up office John Duncan had found that 'the skins of animals collected by the Tradescants had fallen into total decay', resulting in the discarding of further elements of the founding collection and their replacement with freshly prepared specimens – more richly endowed, no doubt, with visual and scientific interest than the dusty, worm-eaten specimens they replaced but lacking the irreplaceable historical interest of the latter. Already by the end of his second year in office Duncan could claim that virtually the whole of the greatly expanded collection of birds were gifts from himself and from his friends. With continued industry on the part of the two brothers, 'New Cabinets covering entirely each end of the Museum' were installed, and glazed cases for 'Rarities formerly uncovered & unarranged' were acquired. Existing cases were repaired and refurbished: where appropriate their contents were identified by legends applied in gold paint and the name of every specimen was 'conspicuously affixed'. No one could have doubted that the Ashmolean was once again functioning as a tightly-run and purposeful institution, although the intellectual framework conceived for it by its founder now gave way to a programme in which scientific endeavour was shot through with evangelising zeal.

However successful this transformation, developments taking place elsewhere in Oxford were soon to overtake the Museum. In particular, the growing importance attributed in the University curriculum to the natural sciences (in which the Ashmolean itself had played an honourable role) resulted in a decision to establish a dedicated Natural Science Museum (opened in 1860 and surviving today as the Oxford University Museum of Natural History). Philip Duncan's successor at the Ashmolean, the geologist John Philips, had come to Oxford as Deputy Reader in Geology and also as first curator of the new institution, and had the task of dismantling his predecessors' pious creation so that its contents could be systematically integrated with the collections of the Natural Science Museum. That building contained also lecture rooms and laboratories for the teaching of astronomy, geometry, experimental physics, chemistry, mineralogy, geology, zoology, anatomy, physiology and medicine, reflecting a scope for the study of specialised areas of the natural sciences greatly expanded since Ashmole's day.

Also in 1860 the Ashmolean's important library of books and manuscripts was transferred to the Bodleian Library, while the coin collections were also integrated with those of the Bodleian's coin cabinet. Left behind in the heavily denuded galleries at the Ashmolean, meanwhile, were only the ethnographic and antiquarian collections, together with a few pictures, but these were to form the core exhibits for the next phase of the Museum's development.

Ever since 1828, when an important collection of Anglo-Saxon material had been presented by Sir Richard Colt Hoare, archaeological exhibits had increased slowly but steadily. Under the regime of John Henry Parker (1870–84) and, more particularly, that of his successor Arthur Evans (1884–1908), this element was greatly expanded to fill the vacuum left behind by the loss of the natural

Fig. 6. Archaeological exhibits fill the ground-floor gallery of the 'Old Ashmolean', c. 1864.

Fig. 7. *Guy Fawkes's lantern*, H 34.5 cm, which the would-be regicide is said to have been carrying at the moment of his arrest in 1605, when the Gunpowder Plot was uncovered.

history specimens: a photograph of *c.* 1864 (Fig. 6) shows the ground-floor gallery now crowded with material of this kind. Ethnographic specimens also continued to arrive from all corners of the Empire and beyond, some from clergymen and servants of the East India Company, others from well-known mariners such as Captains Beechey and Lyon. During the 1880s Arthur Evans redisplayed many of the pieces which he was able to relate to the Tradescant collection in cabinets installed on the ground floor, but following the founding in 1883 of a new institution dedicated to the study of ethnography and prehistory – the Pitt Rivers Museum – another round of University rationalisation saw virtually all of the Ashmolean's ethnographic collections transferred to the new specialised museum in 1886. Only a small number of items considered of primary importance to the Ashmolean's own history was retained thereafter for display. In exchange, Evans received the (much less important) collections of antiquities that had accumulated in the University Museum and in the Bodleian Library; the latter's cabinet of curiosities predated even the establishment of the Ashmolean and included alongside some highly dubious items (such as Joseph's many-coloured coat and a piece of salt exhibited as a fragment of Lot's wife), historical relics of more durable character such as Guy Fawkes's lantern (Fig. 7).

Arthur Evans's period of office was to prove critical for the Museum. Under his energetic leadership the antiquarian exhibits expanded at an impressive rate; Evans's own activities in the Balkans and, more particularly, the Near Eastern and Egyptian material collected on behalf of the Museum by the Revd Greville Chester, resulted in a notable expansion of the collections to the point where the building was effectively filled by them. This impressive expansion was crowned by the loan of part of the collection of Renaissance ceramics, finger-rings and other antiquities formed by C.D.E. Fortnum, a loan which, it was made clear, might be converted to a bequest of the entire collection if the University were to demonstrate its support with a reciprocal gesture. Under Evans's guidance, Fortnum's bequest – like Ashmole's before him – was framed in terms that demanded a commitment from the University in the form of a new and appropriately equipped building as a home for the collection. Fortunately, the University had in 1883 acquired a parcel of land to the rear of the University Galleries in Beaumont Street; here the new premises were built and in 1894 the entire contents of the oldest public museum in England, erected to house Ashmole's benefaction, were transferred to their new home.

The University Galleries (Fig. 8), which were to play a central part in the development of the Ashmolean during the twentieth century, had been established in 1845 in imposing quarters in neo-Grecian style, designed by C.R. Cockerell. The principal components of Cockerell's structure were a ground-floor sculpture gallery and a top-lit upper floor designed to receive the University's collection of paintings. At first the sculpture gallery was occupied exclusively by plaster-casts, initially comprising the studio collection of the sculptor Sir Francis Chantrey but later augmented by the heavily restored classical marbles and works by contemporary sculptors in classical style from the collection of Thomas Howard, Earl of Arundel (1585–1646), which had been given to the University in two major tranches, in 1667 and 1755 respectively. On the upper floor the founding collection of paintings, mostly drawn from a picture gallery formerly established in the Bodleian Library and comprising portraits of figures who had played some role in the history of the University rather than works chosen on artistic merit, were in time joined by more distinguished canvases which were to transform the quality of the display. Along with an incomparable collection of Raphael drawings acquired in the early years of its existence, the addition of important early Italian

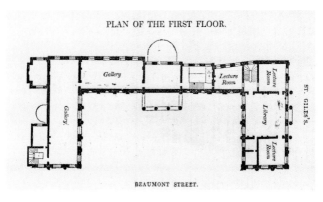

PLAN OF THE FIRST FLOOR.

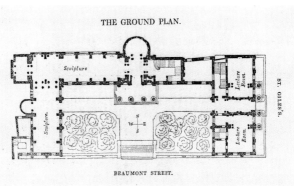

THE GROUND PLAN.

Fig. 8. The University Galleries in Beaumont Street, 1845. The Ashmolean collections occupied an extension to the rear from 1895 and in 1908 the two institutions were merged to form the Ashmolean Museum of Art and Archaeology.

paintings given by William Fox-Strangways, 4th Earl of Ilchester, may be mentioned as important milestones in the development of the collections. From 1871 the Galleries also provided a home for the Ruskin School of Drawing, established in the western wing on the ground floor, and from 1884 the Professor of Classical Archaeology was also housed there. (The latter association survives today, while the Ruskin School moved to its present quarters in the High Street in 1974.)

Following a decade during which the art collections of the University Galleries and the antiquities belonging to the Ashmolean were displayed in close proximity to each other but under quite separate administrations, the two institutions were formally merged in 1908 to form the Ashmolean Museum of Art and Archaeology – the official title which the building and the integrated collection it houses retain to this day. The two founding departments, the 'Antiquarium' initially under D.G. Hogarth (succeeded by E.T. Leeds in 1928), and the Fine Art Galleries, under C.F. Bell (followed successively by Kenneth [later Sir Kenneth] Clark in 1931 and Karl [later Sir Karl] Parker in 1934), retain their separate identities as the Departments of Antiquities and of Western Art respectively.

In 1921 the coins and medals from the Bodleian Library's collection (augmented by those transferred there from the 'Old Ashmolean' in 1860) were reabsorbed by the Ashmolean; initially they were administered as part of the Department of Antiquities, but subsequently were separately established as the Heberden Coin Room in 1961. In the same year the final curatorial building-block was moved into place with the transfer of the Indian Institute's collections to the Ashmolean to form the basis of the Department of Eastern Art, whose area of interest today encompasses much of the oriental world, including the Islamic lands, China, Japan and India.

In 1983 the Ashmolean celebrated its tercentenary. In the course of three centuries of fluctuating fortunes the Museum had been forced to adapt its primary role on more than one occasion. The natural sciences had been banished from the centre of its interests; the material culture of contemporary and recent societies had given way to a focus on more remote antiquity, which, like the fine arts and decorative arts of western Europe and the orient, had scarcely registered in the earliest collections. The balance of the Museum's constituency had also changed: although it continues to play a primary role in the academic life of the University, the wider public – admitted from the earliest days under Plot and Lhwyd – now occupies the foremost place in considerations of presentation. A dedicated Education Service helps to introduce and to interpret the collections to visitors from early school age onwards. At the new millennium, the Ashmolean looks forward to a future no less engaged with contemporary preoccupations than that envisaged by its founder over three centuries ago.

The Ashmolean is renowned for the range and variety of its archaeological collections assembled by travellers or recovered in excavations conducted by British expeditions to Egypt, the Near East and Europe, largely between 1880 and 1970, and by archaeologists working in the Upper Thames Valley and elsewhere in the United Kingdom. Outstanding amongst these are finds from excavations by Sir Arthur Evans at Knossos in Crete (from 1900); by Sir Flinders Petrie (from 1882 to 1934) at numerous sites in Egypt, notably Abydos, Tell el Amarna and Hierakonpolis, and Palestine; by the Oxford-Chicago Expedition to Kish in Iraq (1923–33) and by Kathleen Kenyon at Jericho (1952–58) and Jerusalem (1961–67). Amongst the special collections in the Department, in many cases not from controlled archaeological excavations, a number are internationally renowned: the Greek Vases, the 'Luristan Bronzes', the ancient seals and the Dark Age jewellery. Of great historic interest are survivors of the 1683 foundation collections, shown in the Tradescant Room, together with other objects from the early collections. These include from the seventeenth century *Guy Fawkes's Lantern* (p. 16), the fortified hat worn by Judge Bradshaw at the trial of Charles 1 and Oliver Cromwell's death-mask, as well as some famous native American antiquities, notably *Powhatan's Mantle* (p. 8).

1. *Athenian Pottery Jar (Pelike)*, baked clay, H 40 cm, Rhodes, Greece, 5th century BCE. Scenes of men at work such as this are not very common on Greek pots, most reflecting aristocratic activities. Such pieces are, however, an area in which the Ashmolean is peculiarly rich, reflecting the fact that the Oxford collection was largely formed when the Arts and Craft movement was at its height. Here we see a shoemaker cutting a piece of leather round the foot of a customer. Beneath the table is a bowl of water with which the leather would be wetted before cutting. Above the shoemaker is a rack containing, from left to right, two knife blades with the tangs showing, a knife like the one that the shoemaker is using, and a clicker's knife. A shoemaker's establishment has actually been found near the Athenian agora (market-place). **G33**. NB. The references at the end of each caption indicate the room in which the work is found (see plan of galleries on inside cover for details).

2. *Ceremonial Palette (the 'Two-Dog Palette')*, schist, carved in low relief, 42.5 x 22 cm, from the 'Main Deposit' in the temple enclosure, Hierakonpolis, Upper Egypt, Protodynastic, 3200–3050 BCE, excavated in 1898. This palette was found with a mass of archaic objects, including the *'Scorpion Macehead'* (p. 24), which had been buried within the temple enclosure of the falcon-god at Hierakonpolis, the site associated in mythology with the first kings of Egypt. Many of these objects are of greater than functional size, and this is an enlarged and decorated version of the kind of palette used for grinding cosmetic paint. On one side (see opposite), the elongated bodies of a pair of Cape Hunting Dogs (*Lycaon pictus*) frame combative scenes featuring collared, domesticated hounds as well as wild beasts and fantastic creatures. A pair of fantastic felines with sinuous necks protectively surround the reservoir for grinding pigment, while on the reverse side (see below) an enigmatic figure with a jackal head – a masked man or an extraordinary beast? – plays a flute, to which other animals seem to prance in peaceful contrast to the scenes of combat. **G6**.

3. *The 'Scorpion Macehead'*, limestone, carved in low relief, H 32.5 cm, from the 'Main Deposit', Hierakonpolis, Upper Egypt, Protodynastic, 3200–3050 BCE. Restored from fragments found in the 'Main Deposit' at Hierakonpolis (see also *Ceremonial Palette*, p. 22), this macehead is some four to five times the size of a functional object: a pear-shaped macehead of stone, fitted with a handle bound with leather, was a prehistoric weapon which had already passed from actual into symbolic use before the beginning of the Protodynastic Period. The four giant maceheads found shattered in the 'Main Deposit' may have been dedications to celebrate a royal triumph or jubilee, set up on poles within the temple enclosure. The ruler shown here wears the crown of Upper Egypt and holds a hoe to cut soil, perhaps for the ceremonial opening of an irrigation channel or a foundation trench. The signs in front of him – a rosette and a scorpion emblem on a peg – have led to the suggestion that he might be a 'King Scorpion', but there is no clear evidence for a Protodynastic ruler of this name; the scorpion, of which many models were found at Hierakonpolis, might have been a symbol of power. **G6**.

4. *The Daughters of Akhenaten and Nefertiti (the 'Princesses Fresco')*, painted plaster, 40 x 165 cm, from the 'King's House' at el-Amarna (ancient Akhetaten), Middle Egypt, late 18th Dynasty, 1353–1335 BCE.

In an intimate scene typical of the innovative art of the brief 'Amarna Period', two of the younger royal daughters are perched on cushions at the feet of their mother, Queen Nefertiti; the red sash of her dress falls obliquely behind them, while her foot is seen to the right. The girls are shown bejewelled but naked, with the shaven heads of childhood, the back of the skull extended as always in portrayals of the royal family of Amarna. The fragment comes from the lower part of a mud-brick wall; the figures of the girls' parents would have appeared above, with their three elder sisters standing between them, and baby Setepenre seated on her mother's lap. Other fragments of this wall are in the Petrie Museum (University College London) and the Manchester Museum, and parts of a similar scene from the opposite wall are in Cairo. The room decorated with these groups was part of a small complex linked to the Great Palace and intended perhaps for the royal family's use. The palace itself was the scene of the formal occasions at which Akhenaten conducted the business of his new capital city, devoted to the cult of the sun-disk, the Aten. **G7**.

5. *Statuette of a Scribe of Thoth*, limestone, H 31.5 cm, probably from Ashmunein (ancient Hermopolis Magna), Middle Egypt, 19th Dynasty, 1307–1196 BCE. The god Thoth, whose sacred creatures were the baboon and the ibis bird, was the patron of writing and mathematics and served as the gods' own scribe. The hieroglyphic inscription on the back of this limestone statuette invokes funerary offerings for the unknown scribe who is shown with a sacred baboon seated on his shoulders. The animal is depicted with a pleasing naturalness, but the outline of its shaggy coat and the line formed by its paws across the man's forehead mimic the contours of the wig one might expect to see here – a typical Egyptian solution to the inclusion of an unusual sub-ject within formal artistic norms. The priest, who probably served in the tem-ple of Thoth at Hermo-polis, wears over his pleat-ed linen tunic the leopard-skin which denotes his clerical rank, and carries in his right hand a folded object which may be a bag of writing equipment. His name has been lost with the lower part of the stat-uette. **G6**.

6. *Double-Sided Mummy Portrait*, encaustic paint on wood, 38 x 14.8 cm, from er-Rubayat, Fayum, Egypt, AD 90–110. This thin panel of lime or linden wood, painted in encaustic (pigment and hot wax), is unusual in carrying an image on both sides. Painted portraits were used in Egypt during the Roman Period to confer personal identity on a dead person's mummy, in accordance with the traditional Egyptian belief that preservation of the deceased's physical appearance was essential for well-being in the afterlife. At least some of these portraits – to our eyes highly naturalistic – were painted during the subject's lifetime and may have hung on house walls before being adapted for funerary use. The distinguished historian of Greek art, Sir John Beazley, to whose collection this portrait once belonged, thought that the plain girl on one side might be the sister of the pretty one on the other. The features are so similar, however, it seems that they may represent the same person, softened in aspect and embellished with a mass of fashionable corkscrew curls for the side which had been used face outwards on a bandaged mummy; perhaps the first version was considered too unflattering. **G28**.

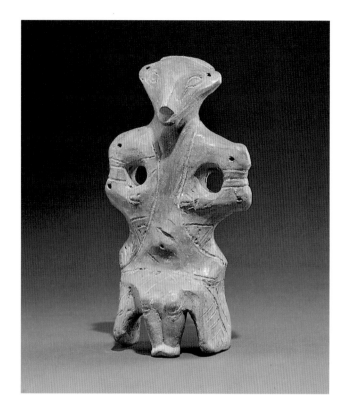

7. *Late Neolithic Seated Figurine*, baked clay, H 15.5 cm; W (max) 8.2 cm, probably from Serbia, early 5th millennium BCE. This figurine is an unusual example of a common class of Late Neolithic objects in south-east Europe. Its style is characteristic of the Vinča culture, and its quality suggests that it belongs to one of the major centres of that culture, perhaps Vinča itself (near Belgrade, Serbia, overlooking the Danube). The 'integral seat' type is known both from Vinča and Tisza contexts, but the pose with hands on hips is a specifically Vinča trait. The face is rather unusual, however, in its sharply triangular outline: this feature has some parallels with products of the Priština group further south. The nose and feet are restored. Holes in the head and arms would have served for the insertion of organic embellishments, such as feathers. **G29**.

8. *Late Iron Age Iron Sword in Bronze Scabbard*, L 80.7 cm; W (max) 6.4 cm, river Thames near Day's Lock, Long Wittenham, mid-1st century BCE. This iron sword is corroded into its bronze sheath. The sheath consists of two sheet-bronze plates with a cast chape at the bottom. At the top, just below the iron tang for the hilt (now missing), is a plate decorated with ornament in the shape of a lyre; the domed rivets are a later addition. Along its length is a fine incised ladderwork ornament. The scabbard may be dated stylistically by its insular ornament to the middle of the 1st century BCE, approximately at the time of Julius Caesar's invasion. The picture below depicts a cast bronze alloy shield, also found at Long Wittenham, DIAM. 39 cm, Late Bronze Age, *c.* 1200 BCE. **G29**.

9. *Gold Necklace*, L 31 cm, found at Nymphaeum, Crimea, prehistoric Ukraine, 5th century BCE. There are few more exquisite pieces of jewellery from the classical period than this necklace. Twenty-two rosettes with acorns suspended from them alternate with stylised lotuses which support small beads. Both rosettes and lotuses each have a smaller rosette attached to them. All these elements are made of sheet gold edged with beaded gold wire, which were originally decorated with coloured enamel. The acorns are highly realistic: the striated cups joined to the smooth glands, the junction cleverly disguised. They were found in a grave at Nymphaeum which contained a silver cup, as well as a bronze wine-strainer. **G33**.

10. *Bronze Age Figurine of Standing Figure with Sheep*, bronze, H 17.5 cm, W 7.6 cm, probably from Sardinia, late 2nd or early 1st millennium BCE. The figure wears a tunic which reaches the upper thigh; the lower portion of the legs is missing. The surface of the bronze shows numerous casting imperfections, due to the inability of the metal to absorb gasses in a closed mould. It was probably cast by the lost-wax method. Sardinia has produced a wide range of representational bronzes, many from the Nuraghi or fortified stone tower-complexes, or other sites of the eponymous 'Nuraghic' culture. The representations often show armed warriors, and sometimes ships: this is a relatively pacific example, conveying the characteristic Mediterranean image of the 'good shepherd'. **G29**.

11. *Cycladic Marble Figurine*, H 32 cm, Amorgos, Greece, Early Cycladic, *c.* 3000–2000 BCE. Many such figurines have been found in tombs on Amorgos, Naxos, Melos and other Cycladic islands of the Aegean. They are now frequently called 'idols', but their true original function is wholly unknown. The present-day vogue for Cycladic art owes much to the interest shown in primitive art by such 20th-century artists as Picasso and Brancusi. The existence of similar figurines in early Bronze Age Anatolia, Crete and Egypt bears witness to the close contact of the inhabitants of the silver-rich Cyclades with other important centres in the eastern Mediterranean, and their role as pioneers of sea-borne trade. **G30**.

12. *Prehistoric Female (?) Skull,* with reconstituted face (much damaged), lower jaw missing, H 15.2 cm, W 16.7 cm, Jericho, Palestine, 'Pre-Pottery Neolithic B', *c.* 8000 BCE. During her excavations at Jericho in 1953, the British archaeologist Kathleen Kenyon found a number of detached skulls with the features reconstituted in clay and painted. Unusually, the eyes here are represented by cowrie shells set horizontally rather than by bivalve shells set vertically, giving a 'sleepy' expression to the face. The recurrent practice of detaching skulls after death for this special treatment in the early villages of the Levant may be part of cults venerating family members ('ancestors'). They include men (young and mature), women and children. Such cults were perhaps intended to strengthen the social cohesion of extended families or groups of families. At a later stage in the Neolithic period at Jericho, plaster and clay were used to make highly stylised statuary of men and women. Examples are displayed alongside the skull in the Museum. **G32**.

13. *Weld-Blundell Prism*, baked clay, H 20 cm, W 9 cm, Larsa, Iraq, *c.* 1800 BCE. This four-sided object, pierced vertically so that it could be rotated if mounted on a frame, is named after the man who gave it to the Museum. It is written in the Sumerian language in the cuneiform (wedge-shaped) script used in ancient Babylonia (southern Iraq). It was written in the city of Larsa to record the rulers of the region from *c.* 3200–1800 BCE ('The Sumerian King-List'). It is a work of literature, not of history as we would understand it. Famously, this list begins with rulers before 'the Flood', in a way very similar to the genealogies of *Genesis* 5 and 11. Then it says: 'The Flood swept over the land. After the Flood had swept over the land and kingship had descended from heaven for a second time, Kish became the seat of kingship'. The Museum has many objects displayed in the same gallery as the Prism, from excavations at Kish in Iraq by Oxford University in 1923–33. **G32**.

14. *Two Hump-Backed Bulls (Zebus)*, baked clay, H 26 cm/18 cm;
L 39 cm/26 cm, north-west Iran, Iron Age I, *c.* 1250–1000 BCE.
Craftsmen in Iran throughout prehistory were inspired by the animal life around them in the ways they shaped and decorated vessels of clay and metal. Outstanding amongst them are the hollow
animal-shaped vessels found in tombs near the Caspian Sea around
the modern town of Amlash. Excavations in a local cemetery at
Marlik Tepe have shown how they were deposited in graves with
rich furnishings in a variety of materials. Who the elite people
buried there were is still unknown. It has been suggested that they
might be the first Iranian-speaking peoples, who had entered
north-east Iran from Central Asia towards the end of the local
Bronze Age from about 1500 BCE. Their descendants were later to
be famous as the Medes and the Persians. **G32**.

15. *Lady on an Ingot,* bronze, H 9.9 cm, Cyprus, 'Late Cypriot III',
c. 1200 BCE. Cyprus was renowned in the ancient world as a source
of copper. Copper ores are found on the northern and eastern
slopes of the Troodos mountains. These ores may be easily extract-
ed and have been exploited for over four thousand years.
Sometime about 1200 BCE a new-found versatility is evident
amongst local bronze-smiths, notably in using the lost-wax process
to cast statuettes. This lady, perhaps a goddess revered by metal-
workers, stands on a copper ingot. The modelling of her body and
ornaments reflects the lost-wax method by which a wax image was
made first, then covered with clay, which was baked to harden it
and melt out the wax. The bronze was then poured into the cavity
to reproduce the image in metal with remarkable precision. This
simple but versatile technique, still in use today, was first used
about 3500 BCE in the Near East. **G31**.

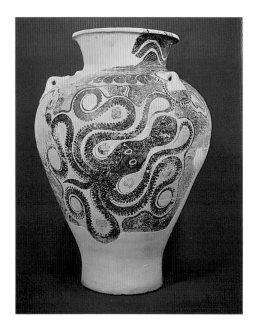

16. *Storage Jar (Pithos) with Octopus Design*, baked clay, H 74.5 cm, Knossos, Crete, Late Minoan II, *c.* 1450 BCE. One of the most important groups in the museum is the Cretan collection, formed largely from the excavations at Knossos conducted by a former keeper of the Museum, Sir Arthur Evans, between 1900 and 1906, and given to him by successive Cretan and Greek governments in recognition of his work. The most characteristic decorative motifs employed in Minoan Crete in the Late Bronze Age were sea-creatures and marine plants. This *pithos* or storage jar is decorated with a sinister but stately octopus and (in the top left part in this view) a *murex* shell, the source of the purple dye which was highly prized throughout antiquity. **G30**.

17. *Statuette of a Lar*, bronze, H 21.5 cm, Roman, 1st century AD. The deity of the home and family is shown dancing forward, his tunic awhirl with the vigour of his movements. With one hand he holds up an ibex-headed vessel (*rhyton*) from which he pours an

offering into the dish (*patera*) held out in the other hand. On his head is a wreath of laurel or myrtle leaves. The eyes of the figurine are enhanced with silver, as are the fastenings at the shoulders and boot buttons, and strips of silver are let into the surface of his tunic. This is the right-hand example of a pair which would once have flanked a Roman household altar, the *lararium*. Many such altars, some complete with their figures, were found at Pompeii. The image of the dancing Lar became popular in the time of Augustus. **G35**.

18. *Amazon*, marble, H (extant) 104 cm, provenance unknown. This figure is a Roman copy of a Greek 5th-century original. Pliny tells the story of a competition for a statue of an Amazon for the temple of Artemis at Ephesus. The artists involved (who included Phidias, Polyclitus and Cresilas) had to choose the winner, and this proved to be Amazon 'which each artist had placed second to his own', namely the one made by Polyclitus. The Ashmolean's Amazon may relate to this project. It is one of many pieces of antique sculpture and inscriptions from the Arundel collection, formed in the early 17th century by Thomas Howard, Earl of Arundel (1585–1646). They were kept at Arundel House in London; inscriptions came to Oxford in 1667, and sculpture (including this Amazon) in 1757. Arundel's collection has considerable importance for the history of collecting in England. **G1**.

19. *Head of a Roman Emperor*, porphyry, H 21.5 cm, 4th century AD.
This fragmentary head of a diademed figure almost certainly comes
from a late Roman imperial relief, although the face, which appears
to have been severely pock-marked originally, has been smoothed
and polished in post-antique times. It possibly represents the
emperor Gratian (359-83 AD), aged about 19 or 20, and may have
been broken off from a larger group of paired tetrarchs (group of
four co-regent emperors). It represents a beautiful example of porphyry sculpture, of which authentic examples are rare (perhaps the
best known examples being the tetrarchs on the corner of the
Treasury of St Mark's in Venice). **G3**.

20. *Roman Bowl*, glass, DIAM. 19 cm, H 5 cm, found at Wint Hill, Somerset, *c.* mid-4th century AD. This drinking vessel is believed to have been made in Cologne, but was found during excavations at a Roman site at Wint Hill, Somerset. Such clear glass vessels were made as cheaper substitutes for rock crystal. This example is engraved on the outer surface, but was intended to be viewed from inside: a horseman and two hounds drive a hare into a net. Around the edge is inscribed VIVASCVMTVISPIEZ in Latin characters, comprising the Roman motto VIVAS CUM TVIS and the Greek PIE ZHCHC, meaning 'Long life to you; drink, and good health'. The decoration links it to other examples with hunting, mythological and Christian scenes whose distribution is centred in the Rhineland. **G35**.

21. *Byzantine Earrings*, gold and precious stones, L 9 cm, 6th century AD. These pendant earrings are typical of the jewellery worn by members of the highest levels of Early Byzantine society which appreciated a vibrant display of costly materials. Such jewellery combines gold and a mix of various coloured precious stones; in the case of the earrings, amethysts and green glass in imitation of emeralds. Pearls may once have hung from the ends. The stones are simply shaped, and displayed to maximum effect. The amethysts have been drilled in characteristic fashion to hang vertically; the 'emeralds' are set in simple box mounts. Similar earrings are worn by the Empress Theodora and the women in her entourage in the mosaic on the wall of the sanctuary of the mid-6th-century Church of S. Vitale at Ravenna. The amethysts used by the Byzantines came from Sri Lanka, the emeralds from the Red Sea. Large numbers of amethysts drilled in the Byzantine manner were exported to western Europe in the 6th and 7th centuries where they were worn strung as beads rather than as pendants. More than a hundred have been found in Anglo-Saxon burials in Kent, some of which are on display in the Museum. **G3**.

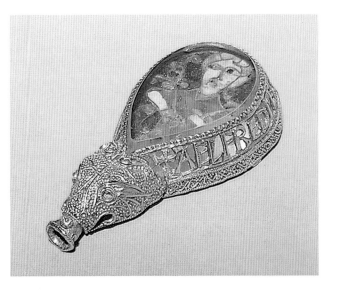

22. *The Alfred Jewel*, gold, enamel and rock crystal, L 6.2 cm;
W 3.1 cm, D 1.3 cm, Anglo-Saxon, North Petherton, Somerset. The
Alfred Jewel is the most precious Anglo-Saxon antiquity in the collection. It comprises three principal elements: an enamelled plaque
depicting a figure holding two flowers or wands; a teardrop-shaped
rock crystal cover to protect the image; and a granulated gold cas-
ing terminating in a dragonesque head and with an openwork
inscription around the edge reading AELFRED MEC HEHT GEWYRCAN
('Alfred ordered me to be made'). Current opinion favours an identity for the figure as a personification of the Sense of Sight. The
superbly modelled animal head holds in its jaws a tubular socket
pierced by a lateral rivet, thought once to have secured a short
pointer, perhaps in ivory. The whole piece is interpreted as an
aestel, with which a reader might read a Manuscript without
smudging it with his finger. The inscription, together with the
exceptional quality of the goldsmith's work, points persuasively to
an origin at the court of King Alfred the Great (871–899). **G35**.

23. *The Holderness Cross*, gold inlaid with garnets, H 4.9 cm,
W 4.9 cm, probably 7th century, Burton Pidsea, Holderness, East
Yorkshire. This delicate piece of Anglo-Saxon workmanship was
purchased in 1999. On a sheet-gold back-plate, cloisonné cell-work
has been built up and inlaid with thin slips of garnet; each of the
stones is backed by a patterned gold foil designed to catch the
light. A prominent central boss is formed by a cabochon garnet
incised with a ring, which originally would have been inlaid,
perhaps with gold. A suspension-loop is fitted to the top. Three
comparable crosses found in England provide a firm context in
the 7th century for the Holderness cross: the two most closely
comparable come from Stanton near Ixworth in Suffolk (also in
the Ashmolean) and from Wilton, Norfolk (British Museum), while
the third (now in Durham Cathedral) was recovered from the
coffin of St Cuthbert, who died in 687. All four date from within
a century of St Augustine's mission of AD 596 and form vivid and
tangible evidence for the early success of the missionaries amongst
the Anglo-Saxon aristocracy. **G2**.

24. *The 'Bodleian Bowl'*, copper alloy, H 25.5 cm, DIAM. 24.5 cm,
13th century, Norfolk, *c.* 1696. A two-handled tripod cauldron, cast
with a Hebrew inscription in relief about its girth, recording that it
was presented as a gift by Joseph, son of the holy Rabbi Yehiel.
The latter was a renowned Talmudic scholar who is known to have
travelled in 1260 from Paris to Palestine (along with his son
Joseph), where he died seven years later. The bowl was for long
assumed to have been carried back to England as Crusader booty,
but recently a document has been brought to light that records the
transfer in 1258 of a property in Colchester from Joseph and another of Yehiel's sons named Benjamin, to a third son named Samuel.
Current opinion favours an interpretation that the cauldron, decorated with fleurs-de-lys and probably of French manufacture, was
presented by Joseph to the Jewish community in Colchester before
his departure for Palestine. **G2**.

25. View of lower floor of Cast Gallery.

26. *The Capitoline Gods Minerva, Jupiter and Juno*, plaster, H 2.71 m, cast of a marble relief from the Arch of Trajan at Beneventum, *c.* AD 114.

Jupiter extends a thunderbolt to the emperor Trajan (shown in an accompanying panel). The relief is a fine example of the grand marble pictures used to celebrate the deeds and virtues of Roman emperors. The cast preserves high-quality detail now eroded from the original.

When the Ashmolean opened in its present building in 1845, casts of ancient sculpture (some dating back to the mid-eighteenth century) were displayed as parts of the interior decoration and as free-standing art-works among the Arundel marbles. They were considered highlights of a visitor's tour.

Casts remained in the Museum until they were moved to the present purpose-built gallery in 1959. The creation of a more systematic cast collection, for academic research and teaching, began in the 1880s with the emergence of the new discipline of Classical Archaeology. Most of the casts acquired before 1914 were of Roman marble versions after Classical Greek statues, while almost all those acquired subsequently were of original marble and bronze sculptures of a broad range of archaeological types.

The Cast Gallery today contains some 900 plaster casts of original statues and reliefs of the Greek and Roman periods. The collection is particularly strong in casts of Classical sculpture (fifth and fourth centuries BCE), but also has important Hellenistic and Roman imperial material.

The upper floor displays casts of sculptures of the Archaic and Early Classical periods (c. 600–450 BCE), and a central focus is an excellent bronze overcast of the famous striding *Zeus from Cape Artemision*, presented to the Gallery by Sir Arthur Evans. There is also a fine series of casts of Late Archaic *korai* (votive statues of young girls) from Athens, together with a large-scale model of the Athenian Acropolis. The colossal architectural sculptures from the *Temple of Zeus at Olympia* are also well represented.

The lower floor displays casts of Classical, Hellenistic and Roman material – from a large collection of *Parthenon marbles* and *Athenian grave reliefs* through to the *Laocoon group* (p. 47) and several colossal historical reliefs from the *Arch of Trajan at Beneventum* (opposite). Important attractions that frame the display are complete casts of two famous winged figures of Victory – the *Victory from Olympia* by Paionios and the *Victory from Samothrace* (original in the Louvre). There is also a separate display of Greek and Roman portraits, tracing the evolution and range of ancient public self-representation, and a wide-ranging collection of ancient gem impressions.

All the casts illustrated are located in the Cast Gallery.

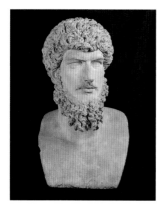

27. *Lucius Verus, Roman Emperor* AD 161-9, plaster, H 83 cm, from Acqua Traversa near Rome. The cast is a virtuoso reproduction of a finely drilled and deeply undercut marble original now in the Louvre. The elaborately curled hairstyle and beard were aspects of the refined elegance displayed by Roman aristocrats of the Antonine age.

28. *Old Fisherman*, plaster and steel, H 1.63 m, Aphrodisias, Caria, south-west Turkey, 2nd century AD. The reconstruction unites casts of parts of the statue now divided between Berlin and Aphrodisias. The statue represents an old fisherman – he originally held a rod in his right hand and a basket in his left. It is a striking re-interpretation of an earlier, Hellenistic figure.

29. (opposite) *Laocoon*, plaster, H 2.33 m, Esquiline hill, Rome, mid-to later 1st century BC. Cast of the famous Hellenistic-style group in the Vatican in Rome with the extended right arm as restored in the 1530s. The original right arm (bent back towards the head) was discovered in 1905. The Trojan priest Laocoon is punished together with his two sons for crimes against Apollo by two man-eating snakes sent by the god.

Coins have been studied in Oxford for at least four centuries, but the various collections in the University – the original Ashmolean collection, the Bodleian and the college collections – are now almost all gathered together in the Ashmolean's Heberden Coin Room. Throughout the twentieth century, the University has been actively collecting, adding to the historic collections and making the Ashmolean's Coin Room one of the finest in the world. It is also a centre of international excellence for teaching and research about coins and medals, which are not only individual objects of great beauty and interest, but also primary historical evidence which speak of ancient kings and princes, and also of the ordinary men and women down the ages who used them. As these illustrations show, the collection is especially strong in the coinages of ancient Greece and Rome, and in the Indo-Scythian and Indo-Parthian coinages which linked the classical world with ancient India. English and Islamic coins from the middle ages to modern times are also well represented in the collections.

All the coins and medals illustrated are in the Heberden Coin Room.

30. *Silver Stater,* DIAM. 3.1 cm, *c.* 525 BCE. The Greek city of Caulonia in Italy, where this was minted, honours the Delphic god Apollo for his role in the city's foundation.

31. *Silver Tetradrachm,* DIAM. 2.9 cm, *c.* 460 BCE. Minted at Naxos in Sicily, a centre of viticulture, this coin celebrates the wine-god Dionysus with a figure of Silenus drinking.

32. *Silver Decadrachm*, DIAM. 3.5 cm, *c.* 390 BCE. This coin was minted in Syracuse in Sicily, and depicts a charioteer crowned by Victory, illustrating the cultural importance of games.

33. *Silver Tetradrachm*, DIAM. 3.1 cm, minted at Alexandria, Egypt, during the reign of Ptolemy I, *c.* 310–305 BCE. A Ptolemaic vision of Alexander (d. 323 BCE) with divine attributes, struck fifteen years after his death. The Macedonian dynasty of the Ptolemies ruled Egypt from the death of Alexander to that of Cleopatra in 30 BCE.

34. *Silver Tetradrachm*, DIAM. 3 cm, minted for Lysimachus, 280s BCE. The Macedonian Athena is shown here, in the ideological service of another of Alexander's successors, Lysimachus.

35. *Silver Tetradrachm*, DIAM. 3.6 cm, *c.* 150 BCE. Bust of Artemis at Magnesia on the Meander in western Asia Minor, which boasted an important temple to the goddess.

36. *Julius Caesar, Silver Denarius,*
DIAM. 2 cm, minted at Rome,
44 BCE. Portrait of Julius Caesar
dating to the year of his assassina-
tion.

37. *Octavian, Silver Denarius,*
DIAM. 2.2 cm, minted in Italy.
Portrait of Octavian at the time of
his victory over Antony and
Cleopatra in 31 BCE.

38. *Nero, Brass Sestertius,*
DIAM. 3.5 cm, minted at Rome.
The coin depicts the arch erected
at Rome under Nero between
AD 58 and 62, to celebrate victories
against the Parthians, a war-like
people from a region south-east of
the Caspian Sea.

39. *Domitian, Gold Aureus,*
DIAM. 2 cm, minted at Rome,
AD 88–9. Portrait of the emperor
Domitian, tyrant and patron of
the arts.

40. *Trajan, Brass Sestertius,*
DIAM. 3.3 cm, minted at Rome,
AD 106. Trajan riding down an
enemy, celebrating his conquest
of Dacia in AD 106. The subjec-
tion to Rome gave the country its
modern name (Romania).

41. *Commodus, Brass Sestertius,*
DIAM. 3.5 cm, minted at Rome,
AD 172–3. The bountiful emperor-
to-be Commodus as Caesar,
making handouts of cash to his
people.

42. *Constantine, Gold Solidus,*
DIAM. 1.9 cm, minted at Ticinum,
northern Italy, AD 315. A highly
unusual portrait of Constantine,
the first Christian emperor, with a
'halo'.

43. *Maues, Silver Tetradrachm,*
DIAM. 2.9 cm, minted at Taxila (in
what is now northern Pakistan).
Maues was an Indo-Scythian king
in the early 1st century BCE. Zeus
holds a sceptre on the obverse,
with Greek legends declaring
Maues King of Kings.

44. *Azilises, Silver Tetradrachm,*
DIAM. 2.7 cm, minted at Taxila.
Azilises was king of the Indo-
Scythians in the mid-1st century
BCE. An Indian goddess is flanked
by two elephants, surrounded by a
Kharoshthi legend declaring
Azilises king of kings.

45. *Azes, Silver Tetradrachm,*
(Hazara), DIAM. 2.8 cm. This coin
of the Indo-Scythian king Azes
(second half of the 1st century
BCE) depicts Zeus wielding a thunderbolt surrounded by Kharoshthi
lettering.

46. *Gondophares, Silver Drachm,*
DIAM. 1.7 cm. Bust of the Indo-
Parthian king Gondophares (mid-
1st century AD), with the Greek
goddess Nike crowning the king on
the reverse.

47. *Wima Kadphises, Double Stater,* gold, DIAM. 2.5 cm. This coin depicts Wima Kadphises, the Indian Kushan king (late 1st century AD), sitting on clouds.

48. *'Standing Caliph', Gold Dinar,* DIAM. 1.5 cm, struck in Damascus, AH 77/AD 695. The coin depicts the Caliph 'Abd al-malik ibn Marwan (AD 685–705). The designs evolved from the Byzantine gold coinage of the period. Note how the cross on steps common on Byzantine coins has been modified to transform the Christian symbol, which would have been inappropriate on an Islamic coin.

49. *'Praying Caliph', Silver Drachm,* DIAM. 3 cm, struck at al-Basra, Iraq, AH 75/AD 693. This coin's design has derived from Sasanian silver coinage. The traditional fire altar of the Sasanian coinage has been replaced with a figure of the caliph praying with raised hands.

50. *Gold thrymsas,* DIAM. about 1.2 cm, Anglo-Saxon, *c.* 640 AD. These coins are part of the Crondall hoard of Anglo-Saxon gold coins dating from around 640 AD. Discovered in 1828 in Crondall, Hampshire, the hoard remains the most important body of evidence for the early Anglo-Saxon coinage. These gold coins may have been the earliest English shillings.

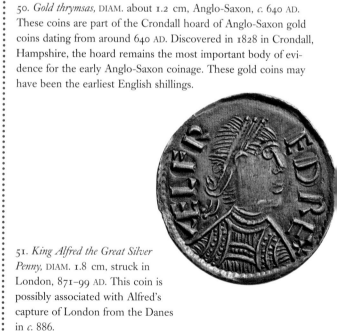

51. *King Alfred the Great Silver Penny,* DIAM. 1.8 cm, struck in London, 871–99 AD. This coin is possibly associated with Alfred's capture of London from the Danes in *c.* 886.

52. *Henry VIII Gold Medal,* DIAM. 4.7 cm, 1545. As a consequence of Henry VIII's break with Rome, he claimed to be the 'Supreme Head of the Church in England'. This medal by Henry Basse records the King's full titles, in Latin on the obverse, surrounding his portrait (left), and Greek and Hebrew on the reverse (right).

53. *King Charles I £3 Gold Coin,* DIAM. 4.1 cm, Oxford mint, 1642–6. This coin was struck during the Civil War, when Charles I made Oxford his headquarters, as London and the Mint there were held by Parliament.

54. *Oxford Crown of King Charles I,* silver, DIAM. 3.7 cm, 1644. The obverse, seen here, shows the city of Oxford depicted beneath the king's horse; the legend on the reverse summarises Charles I's war aims as support for the Protestant religion, the laws of England and a free Parliament.

The Ashmolean's collections of Eastern art are based on those of the University's Indian Institute, which was founded in 1883, and the Museum of Eastern Art, founded in 1946 under the direction of William Cohn. The amalgamation of these collections and the move to the Ashmolean was stimulated by Sir Herbert Ingram's gift of his remarkable collection of Chinese ceramics in 1956. The displays of Eastern art were opened in 1962.

Two large gifts of Islamic ceramics from Sir Thomas Barlow (1956) and of Chinese, Japanese and Islamic ceramics from Gerald Reitlinger (1978) were followed by gifts of Chinese lacquer and seals from Eric North and Japanese ceramics from Jeffrey Story. Funds from these two benefactors have been used to enlarge the Oriental collections. Notable recent acquisitions have included Chinese wooden sculptures and Japanese screens. There have also been important recent additions of bronzes and stone sculptures from the Indian continent and South-East Asia.

Today the Ashmolean's collections of Eastern art are best known for Chinese ceramics and twentieth-century painting (principally consisting of the Reyes collection, given in 1995), Japanese painting and the export arts, Islamic ceramics and Indian sculpture. Its collections are second in Britain only to those of the British Museum and Victoria and Albert Museum.

55. *Sultan Abdullah Qutubshah of Golconda*, gouache painting with gold and silver on paper, 12.5 x 9.8 cm, Deccani school, Golconda, southern India, *c.* 1640. The youthful Sultan Abdullah Qutubshah (*r.* 1626–72) is seated on a low throne on a garden terrace, displaying a radiant nimbus and gripping the hilt of his sword in a martial manner. In reality, he was an ineffectual ruler and his administration was run by his mother. Here the North Indian imperial Mughal convention of portraiture is interpreted by the southern Golconda artist with typical refinement and subtle richness of colour. **G23**.

56. *Seated Bodhisattva*, painted wood, H 173 cm, North China, 13th century AD. This sculpture represents the bodhisattva, or Buddhist figure, Avalokitesvara, known in China as Guanyin, and comes from Shanxi province in northern China. The position of the raised right hand symbolises teaching, and the left, now missing, would probably have lain palm upwards on the left knee. **G19**.

57. *Gui*, ritual vessel, bronze, H 22.7 cm, Western Zhou period (*c.* 1050–771 BCE). The *gui* was one of the principal forms of Western Zhou ritual bronzes, and the more important pieces were supported, as here, on pedestal bases. A six-character inscription cast in the vessel's interior associates it with a region of central north China ruled by descendants of the Zhou dynasty's founder, and a small suspension loop in the centre of the base would have held a small bell. **G14**.

58. *Greenware Jar*, stoneware, H 38.4 cm, North China, 6th century AD. This jar, with heavily moulded decoration in western Asian style, is rare in both its size and its form, though similar ornament appears on some white glazed ceramics and on metalwork and architecture of comparable date. Greenwares were produced in China from about the 14th century BCE until the 16th century AD, at the end of the Ming dynasty. They are perhaps the single most important group of wares in China's ceramic history, and the Ashmolean Museum houses the largest collection of early greenwares outside China. **G15**.

59. *Dish*, porcelain with underglaze cobalt blue decoration, DIAM. 45.7 cm, 14th century AD. Large-scale production of blue and white porcelain began in China in the 14th century and was centred at the kilns at Jingdezhen in Jiangxi province in south-east China. Jingdezhen was the site of the imperial kilns and the source of most of the Chinese porcelain exported to Europe from the 17th century onwards. The 14th century is notable for large forms, particularly dishes, but the mythical beast depicted here, known as a *qilin* or kylin, is a rare type of ornament. **G16**.

60. *Dish*, carved lacquer, DIAM. 54.3 cm, Ming dynasty, early 15th century AD. This dish is rare not just for its large size, but also as an example of an overall design composed of different single flowers, in this case peony, gardenia, camellia, chrysanthemum, lotus, waterweed, peach, prunus and cherry blossom. Lacquer such as this is composed of several dozen layers, each of which must dry before the next can be applied; it could thus take several months to achieve the material before it could be carved, and lacquer carving was a highly skilled technique. **G18**.

61. (opposite) Ren Yi with calligraphy by Wu Changshuo, *Winter and Spring,* hanging scroll, ink and colour on paper, 198.5 x 93 cm, 1891. Ren Yi (1840–96), also known as Ren Bonian, was one of the leading painters of 19th-century China. He worked in Shanghai, and his use of traditional painting techniques combined with colourful, popular subjects established a new style associated with that city. This painting depicts Shoulao, the god of longevity, with a young woman. The calligraphy at the top is dated 1919, and was added by Ren Yi's best known follower, the painter and calligrapher Wu Changshuo (1844–1927). **G13**.

62. Zha Shibiao, *River Landscape*, album leaf, ink on paper, 17.1 x 18.2 cm, 1667. Zha Shibiao (1615–98) gave up his career as an official in favour of painting. He favoured dry brushwork and sparse composition, and often painted much larger scale landscapes in addition to small contemplative works such as this. **G13**.

63. *Plaque of a Yakshi or Mother Goddess*, terracotta, H 21.3 cm, from Tamluk (ancient Tamralipti) in Bengal, Eastern India, *c.* 200 BCE. This exceptionally finely moulded plaque depicts a female nature spirit *(yakshi)* or a mother goddess. Standing erect, she wears a huge and elaborate head-dress and heavy earrings, bracelets and other jewellery. Discovered in Bengal in 1883 and brought to Oxford a few years later, this plaque remains the most famous among the many surviving Eastern Indian terracottas of the mother goddesses. **G20**.

64. *Palette with Goddesses on Sea Monsters*, stone, H 13.7 cm, Gandhara region (Pakistan and Afghanistan), 1st century AD. This palette or toilet tray depicts two Nereids or daughters of the sea god, who ride lively sea monsters. Among the surviving palettes of its type, it is unique in showing two goddesses on sea monsters instead of one. This subject from classical mythology exemplifies the strong Hellenistic influences found in the (predominantly Buddhist) sculpture of the Gandhara region during this period. **G20**.

65. *Image of Ganesa*, bronze, H 10.8 cm, Orissa, eastern India, 16th century. Ganesa, the elephant-headed and pot-bellied son of Siva and Parvati, embodies wisdom and wealth and is one of the most popular Hindu gods, being invoked at the commencement of any undertaking. In this refined Orissan image, Ganesa sits on a lotus-petalled throne, with his vehicle (or associated animal), a rat or shrew, on the base looking up at him. **G21**.

66. *Image of the Buddha*, gilt bronze, H 10.2 cm, Tibet, *c.* 8th–9th centuries. In this early Tibetan image, probably dating from the period of the first diffusion of Buddhism from India, the Buddha is seated in the lotus posture and makes the gesture *(mudra)* of touching the earth, calling it to bear witness to his Enlightenment. The Buddha's curls and *ushnisha* (cranial protuberance) are of pronounced globular form. The edges and folds of his robe are shown in linear fashion. A small projection behind would have secured a bronze backplate or surround, now missing. **G22**.

67. *Four-Sided Caitya Shrine, with Images of Buddhist Deities,* sandstone, H 110 cm, Khmer (Angkor period), Cambodia, 10th century. Acquired in 1999. This monolithic *caitya*, or votive shrine, resembling a miniature temple (*prasat*), bears relief images of benign or protective Mahayana Buddhist deities on its four faces. The principal image (seen here) is the goddess Prajnaparamita, the personification of Transcendent Wisdom. She wears a tiered head-dress and holds in her two upper hands a rosary and a book of scripture. **G21**.

68. *Textile Fragment*, resist block-printed cotton, L 33 cm, India, 10th century. India has been famous for textiles since classical antiquity, but little tangible evidence has survived. Exceptions are block-printed cotton fabrics traded to Egypt in the medieval period; the Ashmolean Museum holds the most important collection of its type, with over 1200 textiles donated by the Egyptologist Percy Newberry. This fragment has a 9th/10th-century radiocarbon date (895 AD +/- 75), which makes it the earliest surviving Indian textile with a distinguishable pattern. Viewed on request.

69. *Mans' Coat,* silk warp ikat, L 122 cm, Central Asia, Chinese
Turkestan, pre-1869. Part of a collection of coats and caps given to
the English explorer Robert Shaw in early 1869 during his travels
in former Chinese Turkestan (now Sinkiang Province). This makes
it one of the few Central Asian ikat collections with a documented
date and provenance; it also is one of the earliest. Viewed on
request.

70. *Figure of a Guardian King*, wood, H 99.5 cm, probably Kyoto, late 12th century. Lack of the arms prevents accurate identification, but this probably represents Komoku-ten, one of the Guardian Kings of the Four Corners. His arms would have been held up in a menacing way, and with the grimacing features, would have been a potent symbol to the viewer of the necessity for good behaviour in this world. **G19**.

71. *Shino Ware Dish* of lobed, subrectangular shape, stoneware, W 24.6 cm, Mino, late 16th century. The Shino wares of Mino, near Nagoya, were the first underglaze decorated wares of Japan, pre-dating the first Japanese porcelain by about forty years. Of purpose-fully irregular shape, they were strongly influenced by the taste of the Tea Ceremony, with its emphasis on almost rustic simplicity. Use of the wheel was abandoned for almost all the Mino wares, for the hand-building technique allowed a more personal touch. **G26**.

72. *Kakiemon-Style Jar*, porcelain, H 35.2 cm, Arita, mid-late 17th century. Overglaze enamelling in Arita began in the early to mid-17th century, before the beginnings of the export to Europe. This exceptionally grand piece, made for export and enamelled by the Kakiemon enamellers, has few parallels in Europe. The Kakiemon pieces are characterised by their brilliant translucent en-amels and the lightness of touch of their design, contrasting somewhat with other contemporary work (Imari) of Arita. **G26**.

73. Attributed to Watanabe Shikô (1683–1755), *Flowers of the Four Seasons*, pair of six-fold screens on a gold ground, each screen W 3.35 m, early 18th century. Shikô, to whom these beautiful screens can be firmly attributed, was a most distinguished amateur painter. Trained, as was usually the case, under a Kanô School master, possibly Yamamoto Sôken, he became the foremost follower of the Rimpa artist Ogata Kôrin, using many of the Rimpa techniques such as *tarashikomi,* the dripping of wet paint on to wet paint to produce the blurred effect so well demonstrated here. The screens read from spring, extreme right, to winter, extreme left. **G19**.

74. *Mosque Lamp*, enamelled and gilded glass, H 31 cm, Egypt, early 13th century. This lamp is a fine example of the traditional form of hanging lamps used in mosques in the Arab world. It bears around the body the name of Sultan Muhammad ibn Qala'un, the Mamluk ruler of Egypt and Syria from 1294-1340. On the flaring mouth it carries an Arabic quotation from the Quran: 'God it is who prays over you, and his Angels also, that He may bring you out of darkness into light.' **G24**.

75. *Dish*, stonepaste with lustre decoration, DIAM. 44.5 cm, Kushan, Iran, c. 1200 AD. Lustre decoration was invented by glass workers in Egypt, probably during the 7th century, and became extremely popular among Islamic potters in Egypt, Syria, Iran and Spain. The

dish depicts a seated ruler with four courtiers around him. Such scenes must derive from contemporary manuscript illustrations, though few of the latter survive. **G24**.

76. *Candlestick*, cast brass inlaid with niello, H 53.5 cm, Turkey, mid-16th century. Brass was widely used in the Islamic world for candlesticks, ewers, basins and other objects of daily use. This monumental candlestick, however, may well have graced one side of the mihrab (prayer niche) of an Ottoman mosque. The Ottomans were particularly devoted to flowers, as the designs they used on their textiles and ceramics vividly demonstrate, and tulips first reached Europe in the mid-16th century through the Holy Roman Emperor's Ambassador to the Ottoman court. In keeping with this taste, their candlesticks developed a tulip-shaped candle-holder: this is a particularly fine example. **G24**.

The Ashmolean collections of Western art extend from the European Middle Ages to the work of living artists and include a wide range of fine and applied arts. Among the most celebrated treasures are the drawings by Raphael, Michelangelo and other European 'Old Masters' (available to the public, to be studied in the Museum's Print Room); the Italian Renaissance paintings, of which the best-known is *The Hunt in the Forest* by Paolo Uccello; the Renaissance bronzes and maiolica given by the Victorian scholar C.D.E. Fortnum; the English silver of the seventeenth and eighteenth centuries; the paintings by members of the Pre-Raphaelite brotherhood; and the paintings and drawings by the Impressionist Camille Pissarro.

The holdings have the character of a 'collection of collections', an accumulation of sometimes highly specialised private collections given over more than three centuries. Examples are the Hill collection of European stringed instruments, the Marshall collection of Worcester porcelain, and the Daisy Linda Ward collection of Dutch and Flemish still-life and flower paintings: each of these collections has a room to itself.

The collections continue to grow by gift and bequest, and a number of major recent purchases have enriched and deepened the collections. The fastest growing area of the collection is now the paintings, drawings and prints of the twentieth century. A new gallery devoted to early twentieth-century art is due to open early in 2001.

77. Giambattista Tiepolo (1696–1770), *Young Woman with a Macaw*, canvas, 70 x 52 cm, *c.* 1760. Tiepolo's vibrant use of oil paint and masterly evocation of texture can be seen in this sensuous and witty cabinet picture. Tiepolo was apparently working in late 1760 on a series of half-length *capriccio* portraits of women for the Empress of Russia, Elizabeth Petrovna, which were said to be lively and beautiful, and this painting, together with *Woman with a Mandolin* (now in the Detroit Institute of Arts) probably belonged to the series. **G43**.

78. Piero di Cosimo (1461/62–1522), Florentine School, *The Forest Fire*, panel, 71.2 x 202 cm, *c.* 1505. Piero di Cosimo enjoyed a high reputation as an artist of great originality and fantasy, and this striking painting is one of his most important surviving works. Closely linked with two panel paintings now in the Metropolitan Museum, New York, *The Hunt* and *The Return from the Hunt*, the picture may have formed part of a decorative scheme on the history of early man and his cultivation of the earth. The magical details of strange beasts and exotic birds here testify to Piero's vivid imagination, while the impressionistic painting of the fire and the beautiful treatment of landscape place the artist in the forefront of the development of landscape painting. **G39**.

79. Paolo di Dono, called Uccello (1397–1475), Florentine School, *The Hunt in the Forest*, panel, 73.5 x 177 cm, mid-1460s. Paolo Uccello was celebrated in his lifetime as a painter of perspective and of animals and landscape. Relatively few of his paintings have come down to us, and *The Hunt in the Forest* is an unusual and beautiful one; it is also a rare survivor from the mid-1460s as a decorative picture of a purely secular subject. Uccello was fascinated by materials and perspective, and underpinning this vivacious richly coloured scene lies a cleverly constructed, logical picture space. **G39**.

80. Mathis Nithart Gothart, called Grünewald (*c.* 1480–1528), *An Elderly Woman with Clasped Hands*, black chalk on paper, 37.7 x 23.6 cm. Drawings by the German painter Grünewald are rare and difficult to date. This drawing is usually dated to the period shortly before he began work on his most famous composition, the *Isenheim Altarpiece*, of *c.* 1512–15, now in the Colmar Museum. The figure represented is the Virgin Mary or Mary Magdalen in a Crucifixion or Passion scene. **Print Room.**

81. Michelangelo Buonarroti (1475–1564), *Ideal Head*, red chalk on paper, 20.5 x 16.5 cm. Michelangelo's ideas were unique and closely guarded, and while he often destroyed drawings rather than let them fall into the hands of the undeserving, he also gave drawings away to intimate friends.

His biographer Giorgio Vasari describes three 'divine heads' of this type in black chalk, made in the 1520s: this enigmatic head study in a warm-toned red chalk shows a figure in a fantastic head-dress turning aside in an abstracted, brooding manner. **Print Room.**

82. Raphael Santi (1483–1520), *Studies of the Heads and Hands of Two Apostles*, black chalk, touched with white, over pounced indications on paper, 49.9 x 36.4 cm, *c.* 1518–19. Cardinal Giulio de' Medici commissioned from Raphael in 1517 a large altarpiece of *The Transfiguration*, now in the Vatican, which was to be a companion piece to *The Raising of Lazarus* by his rival, Sebastiano del Piombo, now in the National Gallery. At the height of his career, and laden with prestigious commissions, Raphael concentrated his creative energies on this vast painting, carefully preparing at the final stage the key narrative details of expressive heads and hands in highly finished drawings. **Print Room.**

83. Claude Lorrain (1600–82), *Landscape with Ascanius Shooting the Stag of Sylvia*, canvas, 120 x 150 cm, 1682. Painted in the last year of the artist's life, this elegiac classical landscape is one of the most haunting of Claude's works. The subject is from Virgil's *Aeneid* Book VII. Ascanius, the son of Aeneas, is hunting in the Roman countryside and is about to shoot a stag. He is unaware that this graceful animal belongs to Sylvia, daughter of Tyrrheus, ranger to the King of the Latins, and that his action will precipitate war between the Trojans and the Latins. Painted in Rome for the picture gallery of Prince Lorenzo Onofrio Colonna, this poetic work was intended as a companion piece to another landscape with a scene from the *Aeneid*, Claude Lorrain's *Dido and Aeneas before Carthage* of 1675–76 (now in the Kunsthalle, Hamburg). **G43**.

84. Jan Brueghel the Elder (1568–1625), *A Vase of Flowers*, oil on panel, 47 x 35 cm. One of the leading members of the first generation of Flemish still-life painters, Jan Brueghel the Elder was primarily a versatile history and genre painter, often on a minute scale on copper or wood. This example, from the artist's maturity, includes a typically heterogeneous mixture of cultivated and wild flowers carefully arranged in a vase of moulded glass. A moth and other insects point to the function of the painting as a *vanitas*, on the transience of life and beauty. **G57.**

85. Sir Peter Paul Rubens (1577–1640), *The Gemma Tiberiana*, oil on canvas, 100 x 80 cm. This is a greatly enlarged copy of a famous ancient Roman cameo, discovered in the 17th century by the antiquary Nicolas-Claude Fabri de Peiresc, in the Treasury of the Sainte-Chapelle in Paris, where it had reputedly been deposited by Louis IX in the 13th century. It depicts Germanicus saying farewell to the Emperor Tiberius and his mother Livia with other members of the Imperial family, including the Emperor Augustus and Aeneas, appearing in the sky. **G43.**

86. Louis-François Roubiliac (1702/5–62), *Model for the Monument to George Frederick Handel in Westminster Abbey*, terracotta, H 98 cm, 1759–62. The composer George Frederick Handel (1685–1759) settled in London on the succession of the Hanoverian King George I. He himself was to become a national institution. He left £600 in his will for a monument, permission for which was granted by the Dean and Chapter of Westminster Abbey in 1759. The commission went to a fellow immigrant, the French Huguenot Roubiliac, who brought to England the virtuosity and vitality of the finest European Rococo sculpture. **G43**.

87. Georg Petel (1601/2–34), *Venus and Cupid*, ivory, H 40.5 cm, *c.* 1622. Petel was established as a master crafts-man in Augsburg before travel-ling to Italy in the early 1620s. Carved from a single piece of elephant tusk, this statuette suggests a careful study of antique marble sculpture, in particular the *Venus Felix* in the Belvedere Courtyard at the Vatican in Rome. **G43**.

88. *Sweetmeat Dish*, soft-paste porcelain, DIAM. 16 cm, English, Worcester porcelain factory, *c.* 1760. The Worcester porcelain factory was founded in 1751, at the height of the European fash-ion for porcelain manufac-ture. It became the most suc-cessful of all English porce-lain factories; production has continued in Worcester, under various owners, to the present day. This dish is an example of the design known as the 'Blind Earl pattern' after the 6th Earl of Coventry. **G10**.

89. *'Monteith' Bowl*, silver, DIAM. 29.2 cm, London, 1684–5, mark of George Garthorne. Acquired in 2000. The Oxford diarist Anthony à Wood noted in 1684 that such bowls, notched at the rim to hold glasses, were jocularly known as 'monteiths' after 'a fantasticall Scot called Monsieur Monteigh, who wore the bottom of his coat so notched'. The bowl bears engraved arms of the Mildmay family and flat-chased decoration of figures in the chinoiserie taste. **G52**.

90. Nicolas Poussin (1594–1665), *The Exposition of Moses*, canvas, 149.5 x 204.5 cm, 1654. Poussin explored the theme of anguish and pain, with the dawning of hope, in this memorable depiction of a Biblical story (*Exodus* 2: 2–4). Pharaoh had charged that all Hebrew newborn sons were to be cast into the river Nile and drowned. Moses's mother put her baby into an ark of bullrushes, strongly made for preservation; his sister stood far off and watched while Pharaoh's daughter came to the river with her maidens to bathe, and rescued the child, naming him Moses. **G43**.

91. *Plate with Hercules and the Hydra*, tin-glazed pottery (maiolica), DIAM. 32.2 cm, workshop of Giorgio Andreoli, Gubbio, Italy, *c.* 1520. In a perspective landscape, the Greek hero Hercules battles the monstrous many-headed Hydra. The design is taken from an engraving which probably reflects one of the most celebrated lost works of Renaissance art, the frescoes by the Pollaiuolo brothers in the Palazzo Medici, Florence. Maestro Giorgio's workshop made a speciality of applying metallic lustre to maiolica. This is an early example of *istoriato* (narrative painted) maiolica in which the whole surface of a plate is used like a canvas as a surface for painting. C.D.E. Fortnum, the donor of most of the Ashmolean's maiolica collection, was the foremost scholar of the subject in 19th-century Europe. **G53**.

92. *Pan Listening to Echo*, bronze, the eyes silvered, H 20.2 cm, perhaps by Desiderio da Firenze, Padua or Venice, Italy, *c.* 1520–40. The Greek god Pan pauses from playing his pipes to hear the voice of Echo; the subject is from a poem by the Tuscan poet Angelo Poliziano. This exquisitely lyrical example of Renaissance bronze casting in the ancient Greek and Roman tradition is in fact a functional object, an inkwell. **G53**.

93. *Ewer*, imitation porcelain, H 18.5 cm, Medici court workshop, Florence, Italy, *c.* 1575–87. Chinese porcelain was treasured as a great rarity in Medieval Europe, but by the 16th century considerable quantities were being imported into Europe. Various attempts

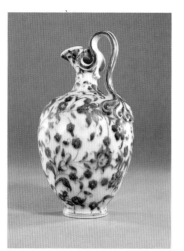

were made in Renaissance Italy to imitate its seemingly magical hardness and translucency. The earliest such attempts of which examples are known to have survived were made in a workshop in Florence patronised by the Medici, Grand Dukes of Tuscany. 'Medici porcelain', of which about 70 examples survive around the world, is one of the rarest and most highly valued of all types of ceramics. **G53**.

94. Antonio Stradivarius (*c.* 1644–1737), *'The Messiah' Violin*, L 59.3 cm, 1716. This violin is characteristic of the larger, flatter instruments which Stradivarius began to make in his native Cremona in the early 18th century, the maker's golden period. Unlike most old violins, it has rarely been played and survives in a remarkable state of preservation. It owes its name *'The Messiah'* to a 19th-century owner who was always promising to show it, but was reluctant to let it appear. **G42**.

95. Michael Rysbrack (1694–1770), *Edward Salter Aged Six*, terracotta overlaid with putty-coloured paint, H 41.9 cm, 1748. Acquired in 1999. Rysbrack was responsible for the enormous popularity of the portrait bust in the first half of the 18th century in this country, and produced a group of child portraits, a number of them of children of the professional middle classes. Edward was the son of Thomas Salter, Clerk to the accounts department of the Royal Household. He died in 1812. **G55**.

96. Samuel Palmer (1805–81), *Early Morning*, pen and brush in dark brown ink mixed with gum, varnished, on paper, 18.8 x 23.2 cm, 1825. This is one of a unique group of six drawings in the Ashmolean, all of the same date and in the same unconventional technique, which constitute Palmer's most original achievement. They were probably made in the village of Shoreham, where the artist founded the group of 'Ancients' dedicated to the ideals of Poetry and Sentiment, and express his intensely personal vision of a neo-Platonic paradise. **Print Room.**

97. Sir John Everett Millais (1829–96), *The Return of the Dove to the Ark*, oil on canvas, 85 x 55 cm, 1851. The wives of the sons of Noah hold the dove that had earlier been released from the ark and had brought back a sprig of olive, showing that the waters of the flood were abating. Shown at the Royal Academy in 1851, where it was much admired by John Ruskin, this is one of the most brilliant and successful of the early Pre-Raphaelite paintings. It was bought by Thomas Combe, the Printer to the University of Oxford, and bequeathed to the Ashmolean by his widow in 1893. **G56**.

98. Camille Pissarro (1830–1903), *Le Jardin des Tuileries, Temps de Pluie*, oil on canvas, 65 x 92 cm, 1899. In his final years, Pissarro painted several series of canvases of the same urban subject, at different seasons and different times of the day. One of the last and largest series, painted in the winters of 1899 and 1900, shows the view from the Paris apartment he rented at 204, rue de Rivoli, overlooking the Tuileries Gardens. In these works, he explored the geometrical compositions created by the relationship between the streets and buildings and the strictly regimented nature of Le Nôtre's parterres. **G45**.

99. Vincent Van Gogh (1853–90), *The Restaurant de la Sirène at Asnières*, oil on canvas, 53 x 65 cm, 1887. Van Gogh moved to Paris in 1886, and was profoundly affected by contemporary Impressionist paintings; he adopted their light colours and broken brushstrokes and to some extent their subject matter, hoping to break into the art market. Asnières was a riverside suburb popular with pleasure-seeking Parisians and Impressionist artists, and Van Gogh made two paintings in the summer of 1887 showing the large Restaurant de la Sirène, near the bridge over the Seine. They illustrate his exhilaration in the newly discovered technique, and are economically painted in short parallel brushstrokes of brilliant colour. **G45**.

100. Pablo Picasso (1881–1974), *Blue Roofs, Paris*, oil on millboard, 40 x 60 cm, 1901. This early work by Picasso is an exciting transitional work and may be precisely located and dated to the 19-year-old Spanish painter's second visit to Paris, in May 1901, when he stayed at 130 Boulevard de Clichy, and settled on his mother's name, the name that came to dominate the art of the 20th century. The limited palette of blue, yellow and white is a precursor of what became known as Picasso's 'Blue Period'. **G45**.

101. Stanley Spencer RA (1891–1959), *Cows at Cookham*, oil on canvas, 76 x 51 cm, 1936. Rarely is an artist so closely identified with one place as is Spencer with the Berkshire village of Cookham, halfway between Oxford and London as the river Thames flows. Known as 'Cookham' by his fellow students at the Slade School of Art, he always returned to his roots for inspiration. Regarded as a visionary artist in the tradition of William Blake and Samuel Palmer, his greatest work is the Sandham Memorial Chapel at Burghclere on the Oxfordshire-Berkshire border. Here he exorcised his experiences of the First World War in a series of murals, which are both contemporary and apocalyptic. Later he developed ideas for an imaginary 'chapel' dedicated to peace, of which *Cows at Cookham* is one. It represents the month of May and is a celebration of spring and another generation in the everyday surroundings of the Moor at Cookham. **G46**.